Rafael Palmeiro

THE STORY OF THE BALTIMORE ORIOLES

Outfielder Anthony Santander

THE STORY OF THE

BALTIMORE ORIOLES

JIM WHITING

Frank Robinson

CREATIVE EDUCATION / CREATIVE PAPERBACKS

Published by Creative Education and Creative Paperbacks
P.O. Box 227, Mankato, Minnesota 56002
Creative Education and Creative Paperbacks are imprints of The Creative
Company
www.thecreativecompany.us

Design and production by Blue Design (www.bluedes.com)
Art direction by Rita Marshall
Printed in China

Photographs by Alamy (Cal Sports Media), AP Images (ASSOCIATED PRESS),
Corbis (Bettmann), Getty Images (Al Bello/Allsport, Lisa Blumenfeld, Diamond
Images, Focus on Sport, Bob Gomel/Time & Life Pictures, Harry How, Paul
Jasienski, Ted Mathias/AFP, Ronald C. Modra/Sports Imagery, National
Baseball Hall of Fame Library, Doug Pensinger/Allsport, Hy Peskin/Time & Life
Photos, Christian Petersen, Photofile/MLB Photos, Rich Pilling/MLB Photos,
Jamie Squire, Peter Stackpole/Time & Life Pictures, Tony Tomsic/MLB Photos,
Hank Walker/Time & Life Pictures)

Library of Congress Cataloging-in-Publication Data
Names: Whiting, Jim, author.
Title: Baltimore Orioles / Jim Whiting.
Series: Creative sports. Veterans.
Includes index.
Summary: Encompassing the extraordinary history of Major League Baseball's
Baltimore Orioles, this photo-laden narrative underscores significant players,
team accomplishments, and noteworthy moments that will stand out in
young sports fans' minds.
Identifiers: LCCN 2019056664 / ISBN 978-1-64026-296-6 (hardcover) / ISBN
978-1-62832-828-8 (pbk) / ISBN 978-1-64000-426-9 (eBook)
Subjects: LCSH: Baltimore Orioles (Baseball team)—History—Juvenile
literature.
Classification: LCC GV875.B2 W55 2021 / DDC 796.357/64097526—dc23

First Edition HC 9 8 7 6 5 4 3 2 1
First Edition PBK 9 8 7 6 5 4 3 2 1

Shortstop Ron Hansen

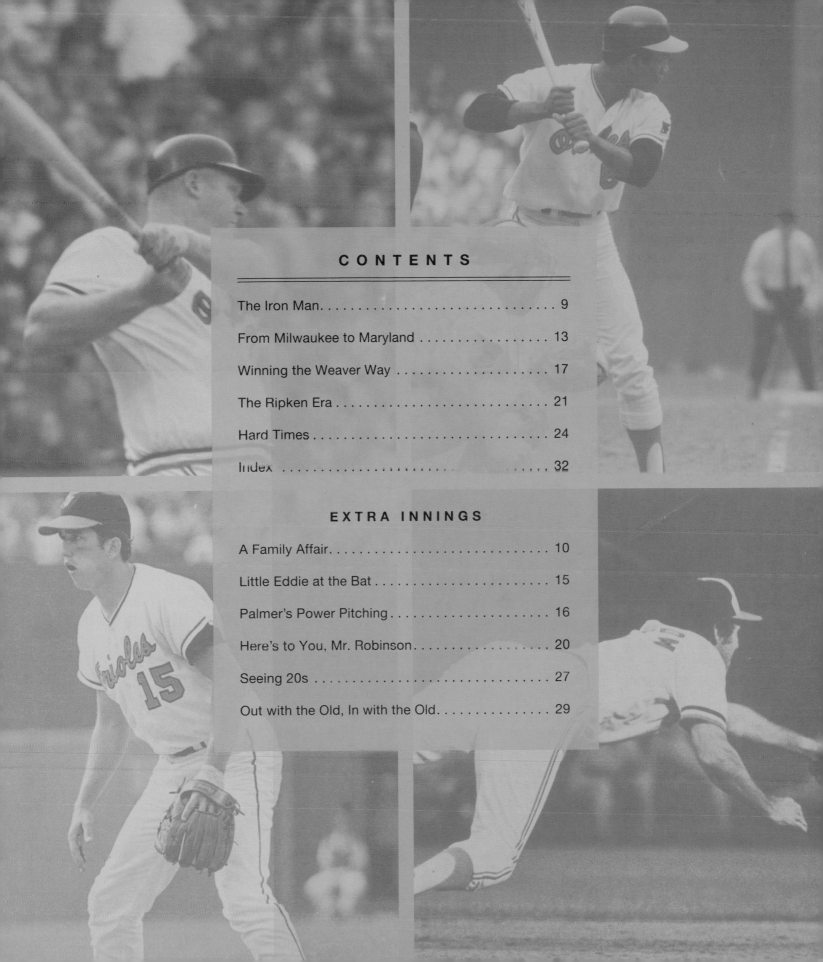

CONTENTS

EXTRA INNINGS

THE IRON MAN

Cal Ripken Jr. trotted onto the field on May 30, 1982. He was a third baseman for the Baltimore Orioles. They were playing the Toronto Blue Jays. None of the 21,632 fans in Baltimore's Memorial Stadium paid much attention to Ripken. His .128 batting average in 23 late-season games the previous year was hardly impressive. On this day, he went 0-for-2 with a walk and a strikeout.

The scene was vastly different on September 6, 1995. A crowd of 46,272 packed Oriole Park at Camden Yards. President Bill Clinton was there, too. Ripken received a standing ovation when he left the field in the fifth inning. He had swatted a home run in the previous inning, giving Baltimore a 3–1 lead over the visiting California Angels. But that was not why fans were so excited. It was now official: Ever since that lackluster day in 1982, Ripken had played in every Orioles game. His streak was now 2,131. That broke the record set by New York Yankees first baseman Lou Gehrig. Gehrig's streak began in 1925. It ended nearly 14 years later. Major League Baseball (MLB) fans had thought his mark was untouchable.

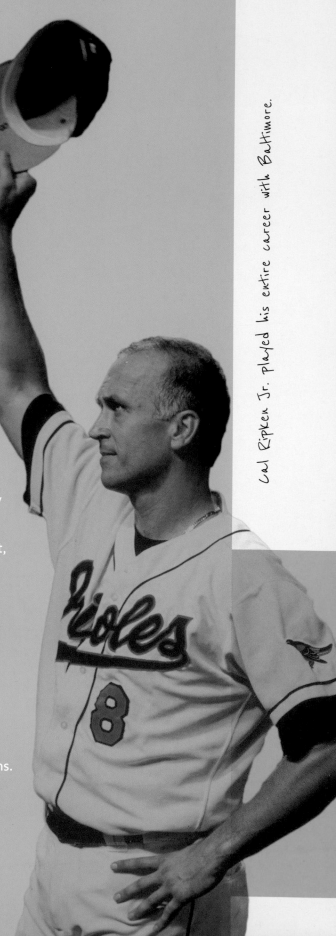

Cal Ripken Jr. played his entire career with Baltimore.

A FAMILY AFFAIR

There have been a number of famous baseball families. Bobby and Barry Bonds and Ken Griffey Sr. and Jr. were great father-son combos. Three generations of the Boone family—Ray, Bob, Bret, and Aaron—played in the big leagues. But the Orioles are the only MLB team to feature two brothers managed by their father. In 1987, Cal Ripken Sr. managed the team. It was the high point of his 36 years with the organization. His sons—shortstop Cal Jr. and second baseman Billy—were both on the roster. Cal Sr. was fired early in 1988. But Cal Jr. and Billy formed the Orioles' double-play combo for four more seasons.

Ripken had long since shifted to shortstop. He revolutionized the position. For many years, shortstops were deemed relatively small players who were "good field, no hit." Ripken stood 6-foot-4. He was an outstanding shortstop. He won two Gold Glove awards, which are given to the best fielder at each position. Ripken also became a dangerous hitter. He finished his career with a .276 average. He smashed 431 home runs. Of those, 345 came when he was at shortstop, a record for the position.

Ripken took his accomplishment in stride. "I never really thought about the streak," he said after the historic game. "It was very simple. I wanted to come to the ballpark, I wanted to play, I wanted to help the team win." He added another 501 games. That brought his total streak to 2,632 games. He finally chose to end it on September 19, 1998. "It was time," Ripken said. "I talked to my wife and decided, 'Let's end it in the same place it started. In my home state. In front of friends and family. In front of the best fans in the world.'" Ripken retired three seasons later. His illustrious career featured 19 back-to-back All-Star nods. He received two Most Valuable Player (MVP) awards. He was named a shortstop on MLB's All-Century team.

FROM MILWAUKEE TO MARYLAND

Baltimore features prominently in baseball history. The legendary Babe Ruth was born there in 1895. Six years later, the American League (AL) became a major league. One of the first AL teams, the Milwaukee Brewers, was not very good. Few fans attended games. The team moved to St. Louis in 1902. It became the Browns. In St. Louis, the team notched 78 wins. It was a 30-game improvement. But from then on, winning was a struggle. The Browns posted just 11 winning records in the next 51 seasons.

One of the team's few good seasons during that period came in 1922. Left fielder Ken Williams belted 39 home runs. That was four more than Ruth. The team won 93 games. But Ruth and his Yankees won the league title by a single game.

In 1944, All-Star shortstop Vern Stephens helped St. Louis win the AL pennant for the first—and only—time. The Browns faced their crosstown rivals, the St. Louis Cardinals, in the World Series. The Cardinals took the championship in six games. The Browns returned to their losing ways for almost the next decade. Attendance sagged.

In desperation, owner Bill Veeck sold the franchise to a group of Baltimore businessmen. The new owners moved the team to Maryland for the 1954 season. They renamed it the Orioles, after Maryland's state bird. Team colors were orange and black, the same as the birds. The Orioles posted a 54–100 record in their first season. The following year, Baltimore showcased three players obtained in a trade with the Yankees. Power-hitting catcher Gus Triandos, slick-fielding Gene

1944 St. Louis Browns

Woodling, and switch-hitting shortstop Willy Miranda were expected to boost the team. Despite the changes, the team's record improved by just three wins.

Baltimore began investing in its minor-league system to develop young players. It became known as the "Oriole Way." The first great player the Oriole Way produced was gangly third baseman Brooks Robinson. He was a defensive wizard. In 1960, the team had a breakthrough year. Robinson batted .294. Rookie pitcher Chuck Estrada had a league-leading 18 victories. Fellow rookie Ron Hansen clubbed 22 homers. He was named Rookie of the Year. The Orioles finished 89–65. It was the team's first winning record in Baltimore.

The Orioles remained strong. In 1965, they traded three players to the Cincinnati Reds. In exchange, they received outfielder Frank Robinson. He was the 1961 National League (NL) MVP. Reds management decided the 30-year-old was past his prime. The trade was one of the best in Orioles history. In 1966, he won the AL Triple Crown. He led the league with a .316 average, 49 home runs, and 122 runs batted in (RBI). Brooks Robinson added 23 home runs and 100 RBI. Jim Palmer and Dave McNally anchored a talented pitching staff. The Orioles clinched the AL pennant with a 97–63 record.

In the World Series, Baltimore faced the Los Angeles Dodgers. The Dodgers were favored to win. In Game 1, both Robinsons slugged home runs. The Orioles won, 5–2. The Dodgers never recovered. Baltimore rolled to a four-game sweep. It was the franchise's first world championship. "To do that to a ballclub as good as the Dodgers is almost unthinkable," said Brooks Robinson. "I'm just glad I was here to see it."

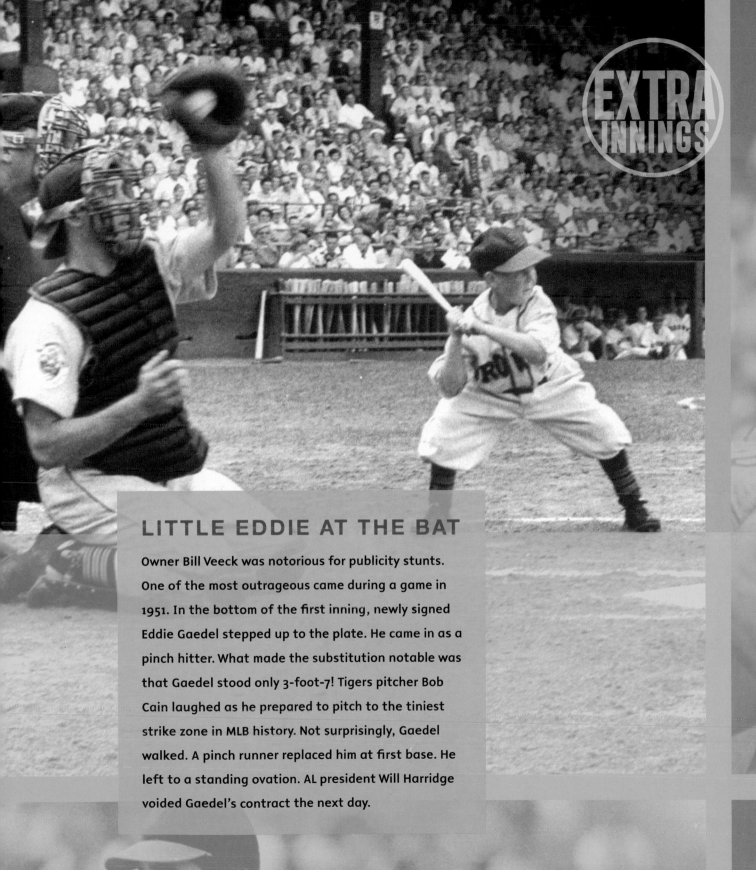

LITTLE EDDIE AT THE BAT

Owner Bill Veeck was notorious for publicity stunts. One of the most outrageous came during a game in 1951. In the bottom of the first inning, newly signed Eddie Gaedel stepped up to the plate. He came in as a pinch hitter. What made the substitution notable was that Gaedel stood only 3-foot-7! Tigers pitcher Bob Cain laughed as he prepared to pitch to the tiniest strike zone in MLB history. Not surprisingly, Gaedel walked. A pinch runner replaced him at first base. He left to a standing ovation. AL president Will Harridge voided Gaedel's contract the next day.

BALTIMORE ORIOLES

JIM PALMER

PITCHER

ORIOLES SEASONS:

1965–67, 1969–84

HEIGHT: 6-FOOT-3

WEIGHT: 190 POUNDS

PALMER'S POWER PITCHING

Jim Palmer holds franchise records for wins, strikeouts, shutouts, and complete games. He also recorded an impressive career 2.86 earned-run average (ERA). In 1966, the 20-year-old became the youngest pitcher to hurl a complete-game shutout in the World Series. He went on to win 20 or more games in 8 different seasons. He captured the Cy Young Award three times. Palmer was known for his high-kick delivery. He was deceptively fast, too. "When you see an easy thrower like him, you get lulled into believing that the ball is coming up there easy," said Angels infielder Dave Chalk. "It's not."

WINNING THE WEAVER WAY

Baltimore declined in the next season. Midway through the 1968 season, manager Hank Bauer was fired. Earl Weaver replaced him. Baltimore's feisty new skipper lit a fire under the Orioles. Fans called him the "Earl of Baltimore." He kept the team in contention. Weaver summed up his style as "pitching, defense, and the three-run homer." He did not believe in "small ball," and its emphasis on stolen bases, hit-and-run plays, or sacrifice bunts.

The AL split into two divisions in 1969. The Orioles stormed through the regular season in the AL East Division. They finished with a franchise-record 109 victories. The Robinsons continued to provide much of the team's offensive power. The booming bat of first baseman Boog Powell helped out. So did speedy center fielder Paul Blair. Shortstop Mark Belanger and second baseman Davey Johnson provided Gold Glove-winning defense. The Orioles swept the Minnesota Twins in three games in the AL Championship Series (ALCS). Baltimore faced the New York Mets in the World Series. The Orioles were heavily favored. But the "Miracle Mets" upset Baltimore in five games.

Stung by the loss, the Orioles came out swinging in 1970. They went 108–54. Baltimore again topped the AL East. It again defeated the Twins in the ALCS. The team headed back to the World Series. There, it faced the mighty Reds. Brooks Robinson put on a jaw-dropping defensive show. He also batted .429 with two home runs and six RBI. The Orioles beat the Reds in five games. "Baseball is a

Third baseman Doug DeCinces

team game," said Weaver, "but what Brooks did is as close as I've ever seen one player come to winning a series by himself."

The following year, the Orioles won 101 games. That propelled them to a third consecutive World Series. This time they met the Pittsburgh Pirates. There would be no championship repeat. The Pirates won the deciding Game 7 with a 2–1 score.

The Orioles captured division titles in 1973 and 1974. But they lost the ALCS each time. By 1978, the team had changed dramatically. Most of its big hitters were gone.

A new generation of Orioles stepped up to bat. Eddie Murray was among the best first basemen in the game. Speedy outfielder Al Bumbry was a base-stealing marvel. Third baseman Doug DeCinces was a heavy hitter. Outfielders John Lowenstein and Ken Singleton provided plenty of power at the plate, too. Mike Flanagan and Dennis Martínez led the team's pitching staff. These new Orioles compiled a 102–57 record in 1979. The team was back atop the AL East. It defeated the Angels in the ALCS. Then it faced the Pirates in the World Series. The result was the same as it had been in 1971. The Pirates won the series in seven games.

Outfielder Al Bumbry

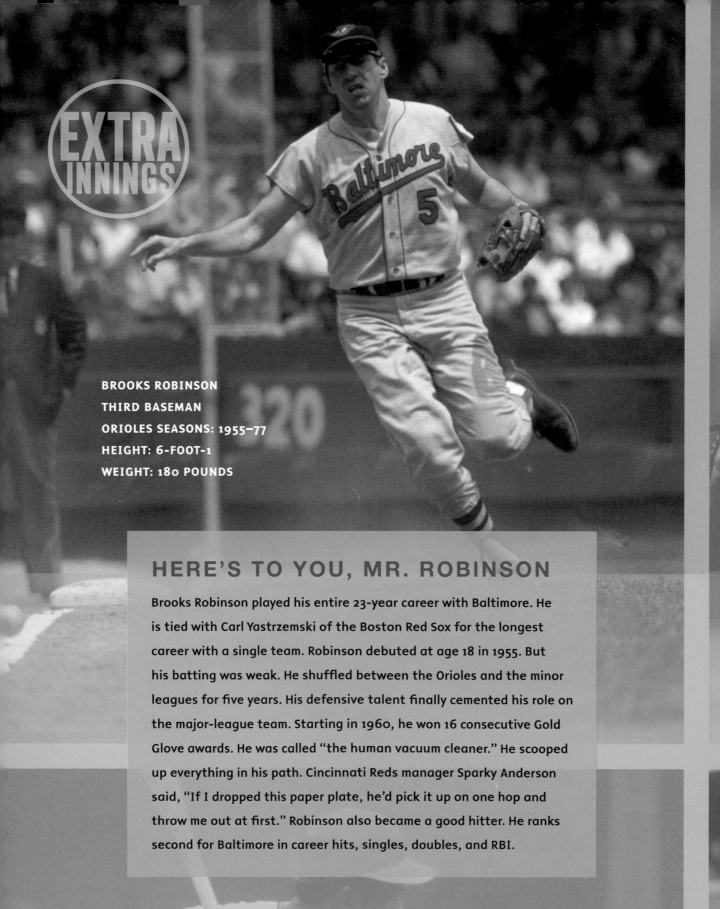

BROOKS ROBINSON
THIRD BASEMAN
ORIOLES SEASONS: 1955–77
HEIGHT: 6-FOOT-1
WEIGHT: 180 POUNDS

HERE'S TO YOU, MR. ROBINSON

Brooks Robinson played his entire 23-year career with Baltimore. He
is tied with Carl Yastrzemski of the Boston Red Sox for the longest
career with a single team. Robinson debuted at age 18 in 1955. But
his batting was weak. He shuffled between the Orioles and the minor
leagues for five years. His defensive talent finally cemented his role on
the major-league team. Starting in 1960, he won 16 consecutive Gold
Glove awards. He was called "the human vacuum cleaner." He scooped
up everything in his path. Cincinnati Reds manager Sparky Anderson
said, "If I dropped this paper plate, he'd pick it up on one hop and
throw me out at first." Robinson also became a good hitter. He ranks
second for Baltimore in career hits, singles, doubles, and RBI.

THE RIPKEN ERA

I n 1982, Orioles fans witnessed a passing of the torch from one Baltimore icon to another. Weaver finished his 16-year managing stint as Cal Ripken Jr. completed his first full MLB season. Baltimore finished second in the AL East, just one game behind the Milwaukee Brewers. In 1983, the team rolled to the AL East title with a 98–64 record. It defeated the Chicago White Sox to win the AL pennant. In the World Series, Baltimore lost the opening game to the Philadelphia Phillies. But the team's pitching staff held the Phillies in check. Baltimore won the next four games. "We have always relied on our pitchers," noted catcher Rick Dempsey. "When you can roll out guys like Palmer, Flanagan, and [Scott] McGregor every day, you're going to win a lot of games."

After that championship, the Orioles experienced a gradual decline. The once-stellar pitching staff began to fall apart. Baltimore set an MLB record when it began the 1988 season with 21 straight losses. Nevertheless, Ripken consistently gave strong performances. Newcomers such as outfielder Brady Anderson and dominating pitcher Mike Mussina did well, too. But as a team, the Orioles struggled. In 1992, the team moved into a new baseball-only facility, Oriole Park at Camden Yards. Inspired by their new nest, the Orioles enjoyed three straight winning seasons.

The Orioles added veteran slugging first baseman Rafael Palmeiro in 1994. Baltimore was near the top of division. But a players' strike in August ended the season early. The team finished third in 1995. Led by Ripken, Palmeiro, Anderson,

Pitcher Mike Mussina

and sure-handed second baseman Roberto Alomar, the team won the division in both 1996 and 1997. But it lost the ALCS both times.

The 1998 season marked the beginning of a new era for the Orioles. The organization had strayed from the Oriole Way. It had fallen into the habit of signing expensive free agents. The team ended up with a huge payroll and few young impact players. It would be an uphill battle to return to the top of the division.

In the midst of the team's slide, Ripken continued to shine. He surpassed 400 home runs in 1999. He made it to 3,000 hits the following year. Ripken became only the seventh major-leaguer to achieve both marks. He retired in 2001. "Cal's retirement brings an end to one of the finest, most noble careers this game has ever seen," said Brooks Robinson.

HARD TIMES

By the time Ripken left, Orioles fans had suffered through four straight losing seasons. The win total declined every year. Right fielder Jay Gibbons impressed fans with 28 home runs in 2002. But Baltimore's downward skid continued. Fans had high hopes in 2004. The Orioles acquired hot-hitting catcher Javy López. They also added smooth shortstop Miguel Tejada.

The additions paid immediate dividends. López hit .316 and bashed 23 home runs. Tejada led the major leagues with 150 RBI. Yet Baltimore finished 78–84.

Shortstop Miguel Tejada

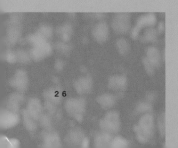

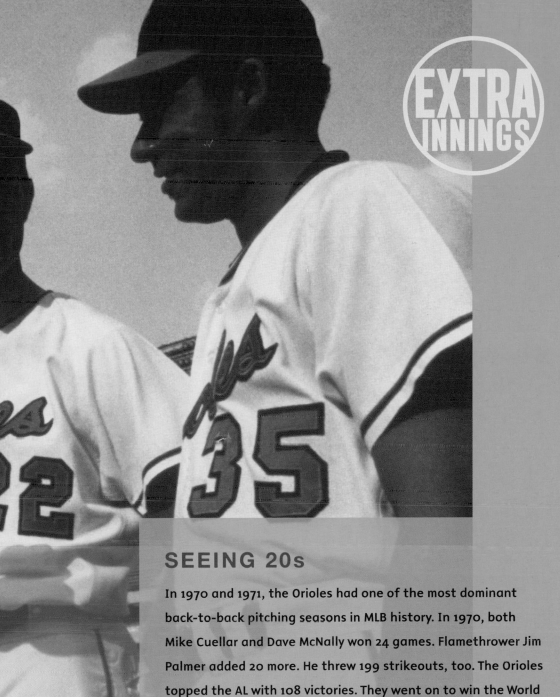

SEEING 20s

In 1970 and 1971, the Orioles had one of the most dominant back-to-back pitching seasons in MLB history. In 1970, both Mike Cuellar and Dave McNally won 24 games. Flamethrower Jim Palmer added 20 more. He threw 199 strikeouts, too. The Orioles topped the AL with 108 victories. They went on to win the World Series. The next year, McNally led the staff with 21 wins. Cuellar and Palmer each threw 20. New addition Pat Dobson made 1971 even better. He was a curveball specialist. Dobson also hurled 20 victories. The Orioles joined the 1920 Chicago White Sox as the only teams with four 20-game winning pitchers.

BALTIMORE ORIOLES

"This is a good, good ballclub," manager Lee Mazzilli insisted. "This is a club that can compete with any team in the league."

Mazzilli was wrong. The team won 74 games in 2005. It had just 70 wins in 2006. After that, the Orioles failed to reach 70 wins for the next 5 years. Their losing streak stretched to 14 seasons. But as outfielder Adam Jones explained, "[Baltimore] has been kind of the hidden city over the last decade…. It's young and raw, but I think we have a very good team." Unlike Mazzilli, he was right.

Baltimore confounded all expectations in 2012. The Orioles flipped their 2011 record of 69–93 to 93–69. Jones had 32 homers. Catcher Matt Wieters added 23 more. Shortstop J. J. Hardy hit 22. All three players earned a Gold Glove. The Orioles made their first playoff appearance in 15 years. They beat the Texas Rangers in the Wild Card game. They took on the Yankees in the AL Division Series (ALDS). But New York prevailed, three games to two. The following season, fielder Chris Davis led the major leagues with 53 home runs. Still, the 85–77 Orioles fell short of the playoffs.

In 2014, Baltimore tallied a 96–66 mark. It won the AL East for the first time since 1997. The team swept the Detroit Tigers in the ALDS. But the Kansas City Royals swept the Orioles in the ALCS. After ending the following season 81–81, they rebounded to win 89 games in 2016. The key was an exceptional bullpen. Closer Zach Britton had 47 saves and a microscopic 0.54 ERA that season. The team played in the Wild Card game against Toronto. But the Blue Jays used a three-run walkoff home run in the 11th inning to win the game. Baltimore's season was over.

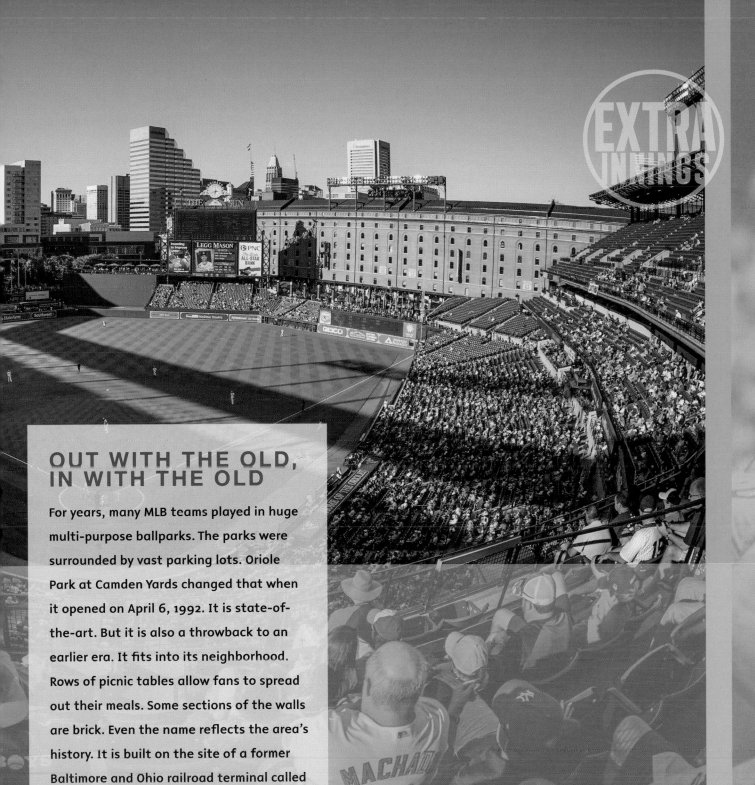

OUT WITH THE OLD, IN WITH THE OLD

For years, many MLB teams played in huge multi-purpose ballparks. The parks were surrounded by vast parking lots. Oriole Park at Camden Yards changed that when it opened on April 6, 1992. It is state-of-the-art. But it is also a throwback to an earlier era. It fits into its neighborhood. Rows of picnic tables allow fans to spread out their meals. Some sections of the walls are brick. Even the name reflects the area's history. It is built on the site of a former Baltimore and Ohio railroad terminal called Camden Yards. Just beyond the right field fence is an old B&O warehouse. Since it opened, Camden Yards has influenced the construction of every new ballpark.

BALTIMORE ORIOLES

Pitcher Dylan Bundy

During this five-season run of success, the Orioles won more games than any other AL team. Baltimore appeared to be on a roll at the start of the 2017 season. It began 22–10. But the team stumbled the rest of the way. It was still in the Wild Card race in early September. But after a 4–19 finish, the team's record was a disappointing 75–87.

That set the stage for a dismal 2018. The team traded its best players in an effort to rebuild. It won just 47 games. That made it the second-worst season in team history. Baltimore were a whopping 61 games behind the division-leading Boston Red Sox. The bad times continued in 2019. The Orioles finished 54–108. Yet again, they finished at the bottom of the AL East.

Baltimore has had many good teams in the course of its long history. Through 2019, seven made it to the World Series. Three hoisted baseball's greatest prize. As the Orioles take flight each season in Camden Yards, fans look forward to the day when orange and black will be championship colors again.

Right fielder Trey Mancini

INDEX